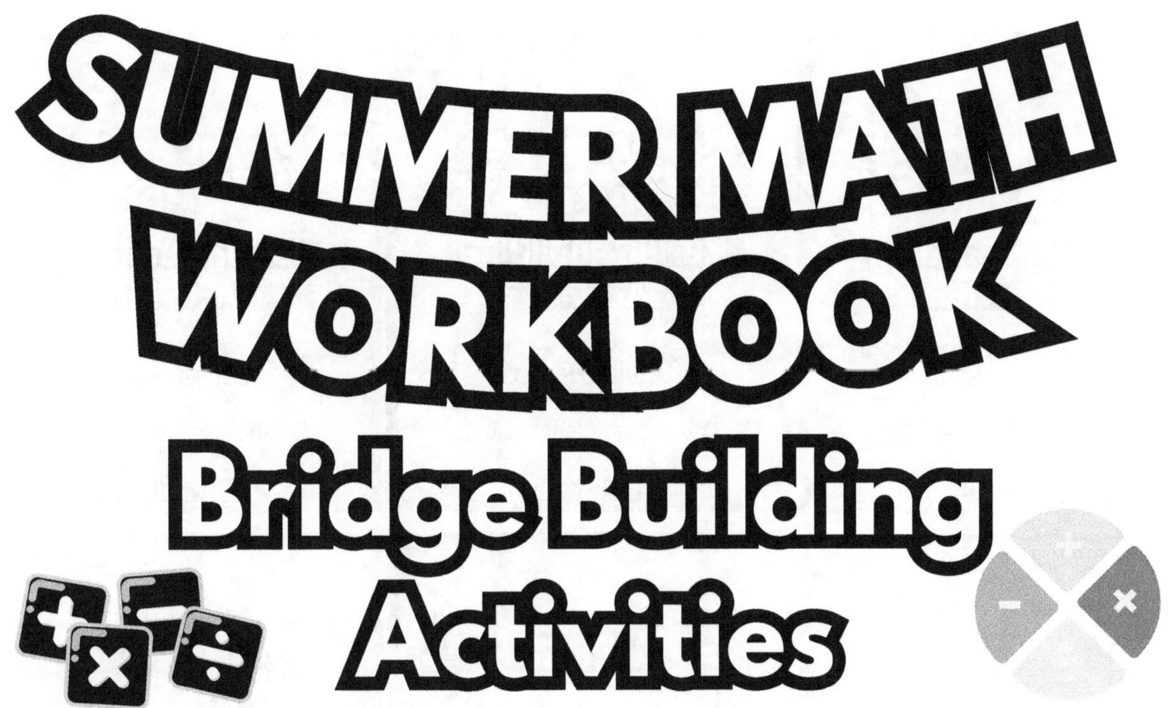

SUMMER MATH WORKBOOK
Bridge Building Activities

Grade
1 → 2
SUMMER MATH
WORKBOOK
Bridge Building
Activities
Number Sense
Addition and Subtraction
Place Value

Grade
2 → 3
SUMMER MATH
WORKBOOK
Bridge Building
Activities
Number Sense
Addition and Subtraction
Place Value

Grade
3 → 4
SUMMER MATH
WORKBOOK
Bridge Building
Activities
Number Sense
Addition and Subtraction
Place Value

Grade
4 → 5
SUMMER MATH
WORKBOOK
Bridge Building
Activities
Multiplication and Division
Place Value and Units
Fractions and Geometry

Grade
5 → 6
SUMMER MATH
WORKBOOK
Bridge Building
Activities
Multiplication and Division
Factors and Multiples
Fractions and Geometry

Grade
6 → 7
SUMMER MATH
WORKBOOK
Bridge Building
Activities
Arithmetic
Algebra
Geometry and Statistics

Grade
7 → 8
SUMMER MATH
WORKBOOK
Bridge Building
Activities
Ratio and Percentage
Algebra and Cartesian Plane
Geometry and Statistics

Grade
8 → 9
SUMMER MATH
WORKBOOK
Bridge Building
Activities
Ratio and Percentage
Algebra
Geometry and Graphing

Grade
9 → 10
SUMMER MATH
WORKBOOK
Bridge Building
Activities
Factoring and Distributing
Algebra
Geometry and Graphing

Introduction

As parents and educators, we understand the pivotal role that mathematics plays in shaping a child's academic journey and future success. Yet, the path to mathematical proficiency can often seem daunting, filled with challenges and complexities. That's where the transformative power of Summer Bridge Building Activities books comes into play, illuminating the way forward with clarity, precision, and purpose.

Summer vacation is a time for rest and relaxation, but it also presents the risk of the "summer slide," where students lose some of the academic gains they made during the school year. Summer Bridge Building Activities books are specifically designed to tackle this challenge, ensuring that your child stays academically engaged and prepared for the upcoming school year. These books provide a seamless bridge from one grade to the next, reinforcing essential skills and introducing new concepts that will give your child a head start.

Imagine your child eagerly diving into the pages of a Summer Bridge Building Activities book, greeted by clear, engaging content that demystifies complex mathematical concepts. With each turn of the pages, they embark on a journey of discovery, encountering thoughtfully curated practice questions that reinforce learning and sharpen problem-solving skills. As they unveil the answers to those questions, a sense of accomplishment blossoms within them — a tangible reward for their hard work and dedication.

Summer Bridge Building Activities books transcend traditional educational tools; they are meticulously crafted to build a deep and enduring understanding of mathematics. These books follow a sequential and logical progression, starting from fundamental principles and advancing to sophisticated problem-solving strategies. Each chapter is designed to build on the previous one, ensuring a solid and comprehensive foundation for future learning.

Parents, we yearn for nothing more than to see our children thrive academically and personally. We want to witness the spark of inspiration ignited within them as they overcome academic challenges with confidence and poise. Summer Bridge Building Activities books serve as indispensable partners in this noble endeavor, offering not just practice questions but the keys to unlocking a world of academic and personal opportunities.

Visualize the pride on your child's face as they master a challenging math concept, the joy they experience when their efforts yield results, and the confidence they gain with each success. These pages are designed to make learning math a positive, enriching, and deeply rewarding experience that will benefit them throughout their academic journey and beyond.

For educators, Summer Bridge Building Activities books are invaluable allies in the quest to cultivate mathematical proficiency in the classroom. Accompanied by comprehensive guides and readily available answers, instructors can focus on mentoring and nurturing their students, secure in the knowledge that these books provide a robust framework for effective learning.

Within the pages of Summer Bridge Building Activities books lies not just the promise of academic excellence, but the seeds of a brighter future. By integrating these resources into your child's summer routine, you are bestowing upon them the gifts of confidence, curiosity, and a lifelong love of learning.

Invest in your child's future today with Summer Bridge Building Activities books — because every great journey begins with a single step, and this step can change everything. Keep the momentum of learning alive over the summer, and watch your child soar to new academic heights.

Contents

Grade 7 - 9
PRE ALGEBRA WORKBOOK
BRIDGE BUILDING
ACTIVITIES
Equations, Inequalities and Expressions
Linear Equations Graphing and Slope
System of Equations Quadratic Equations

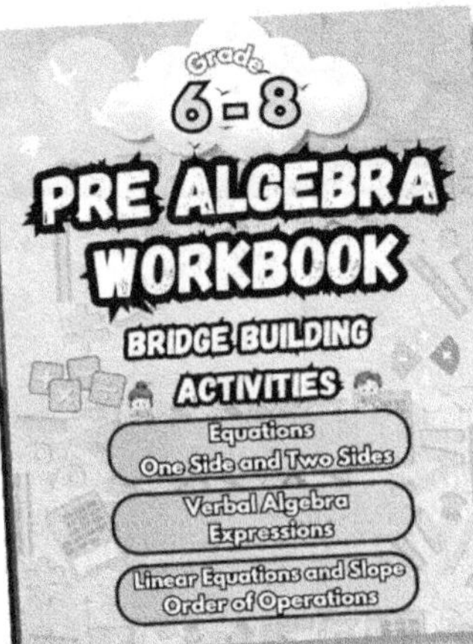
Grade 6 - 8
PRE ALGEBRA WORKBOOK
BRIDGE BUILDING
ACTIVITIES
Equations One Side and Two Sides
Verbal Algebra Expressions
Linear Equations and Slope Order of Operations

Grade 5 - 6
PRE ALGEBRA WORKBOOK
BRIDGE BUILDING
ACTIVITIES
Integers, Mixed Numbers Decimals and Fractions
Place Value Exponents and Roots
Percentage and Ratio Word Problems

PRE ALGEBRA WORKBOOK
for
Beginners
Integers Fractions, Mixed Numbers
Place Value Exponents and Roots
Percentage Ratio Conversion

PRE ALGEBRA WORKBOOK
for
Adults
Integers Percent and Ratio
Equations, Inequalities Expressions
Order of Operations

Grade 7 - 8
PRE ALGEBRA WORKBOOK
BRIDGE BUILDING
ACTIVITIES
Equations, Inequalities and Expressions
Verbal Algebra Expressions
Percent and Ratio Word Problems

Grade 9 - 10
PRE ALGEBRA WORKBOOK
BRIDGE BUILDING
ACTIVITIES
Equations and Inequalities Verbal Algebra
Linear and Quadratic Equations
System of Equations Polynomials

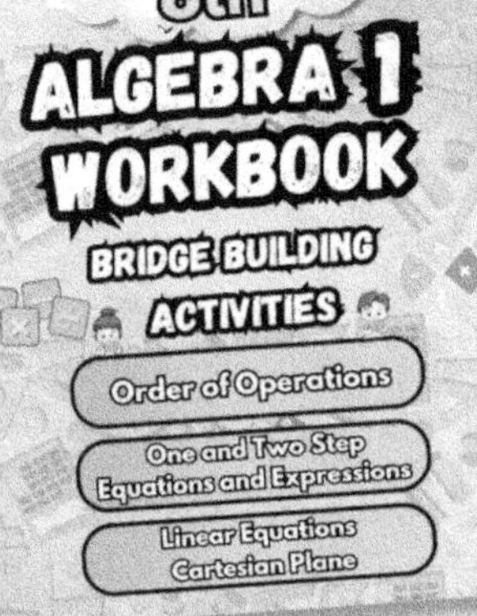
Grade 8th
ALGEBRA 1 WORKBOOK
BRIDGE BUILDING
ACTIVITIES
Order of Operations
One and Two Step Equations and Expressions
Linear Equations Cartesian Plane

Grade 7 - 9
ALGEBRA 1 WORKBOOK
BRIDGE BUILDING
ACTIVITIES
Integers Order of Operations
One and Multi Step Equations and Expressions
Linear, Quadratic Equations Equations One Side, Two Sides

<u>**Order of Operations (PEMDAS)**</u>

The order of operations, often remembered by the acronym PEMDAS, stands for:

- **Parentheses**: Perform operations inside parentheses first.
- **Exponents**: Evaluate exponents (powers and roots) next.
- **Multiplication and Division**: Perform multiplication and division from left to right.
- **Addition and Subtraction:** Perform addition and subtraction from left to right.

The order of operations helps to clarify which operations should be performed first in a mathematical expression to ensure consistent and accurate results.

- **Parentheses**: Evaluate expressions within parentheses first. If there are nested parentheses, start with the innermost ones and work your way out.

    1. Example: $2 \times (3 + 4) = 2 \times 7 = 14$

- **Exponents**: Evaluate expressions with exponents (powers and roots) next.

    1. Example: $2^3 + 4 = 8 + 4 = 12$

- **Multiplication and Division**: Perform multiplication and division from left to right.

    1. Example: $2 \times 3 + 4 = 6 + 4 = 10$

    2. Example: $6 \div 2 \times 3 = 3 \times 3 = 9$

- **Addition and Subtraction**: Perform addition and subtraction from left to right.

    1. Example: $2 + 3 \times 4 = 2 + 12 \ = 14$

    2. Example: $10 - 4 \div 2 = 10 - 2 = 8$

Order of Operations

1. $2 \times 5 =$

2. $7 \times 2 =$

3. $6 + 3 + 6 + 10 =$

4. $(8^2) \times (10^2) + 4 =$

5. $2 + 4 + 8 =$

6. $(9 + 9)^2 =$

7. $5 + 1 + 8 =$

8. $5 + 4 + 9 =$

9. $(8 + 4)^2 =$

10. $(10 + 5) \times (1 + 2) =$

11. $10 + 4 - 9 + 6 =$

12. $1 \times (10 + 9) =$

13. $5 \times 8 =$

14. $(9 + 2)^2 =$

15. $1 + 9 + 3 =$

16. $8 + 8 - 4 + 6 =$

17. $10 \times (1 + 6) =$

18. $2 + 9 - 6 + 9 =$

19. $1 + 3 - 4 + 7 =$

20. $(4 + 2) \times (1 + 3) =$

21. $4 \times 1 =$

22. $(5 + 1)^2 =$

23. $9 + 2 + 4 =$

24. $10 \times (5 + 2) =$

25. $(7 + 9)^2 + (7 + 6)^2 =$

26. $(2 \times 2) - (1 + 10) =$

27. $4 + 5^2 + 1 + 7^2 =$

28. $(8 + 6)(4 + 7) =$

29. $(1 + 7)^2 =$

30. $5 + 8 + 4 =$

31. $(7 + 1)(9 + 6) =$

32. $2 + 3 + 7 =$

33. $6(5 + 6) =$

34. $2 + 1 + 1 =$

35. $3 + 7^2 =$

36. $3 \times 5 =$

37. $2(3 + 7) =$

38. $4 \times 8 + 7 =$

39. $(2 + 8) \times (3 + 10) =$

40. $(8^2) \times (2^2) + 2 =$

41. $8 \times 5 + 7 =$

42. $8 + 10 + 9 + 9 =$

43. $(1^2) \times (10^2) + 9 =$

44. $4 + 5 + 10 =$

45. $(9 + 10)^2 + (6 + 8)^2 =$

46. $3 + 7 + 5 =$

47. $(6 + 5) \times (3 + 1) =$

48. $(1 + 10)(5 + 8) =$

Solving One-Step Equations

Solving one-step equations involves finding the value of the variable that makes the equation true. In a one-step equation, there is only one operation (addition, subtraction, multiplication, or division) performed on the variable.

The goal is to isolate the variable on one side of the equation by performing inverse operations.

For example:

Given the equation $6 = -3z$, where we want to solve for z.

The given equation is already in the form of a one-step equation, with z being multiplied by -3.

To isolate z, we need to perform the inverse operation of multiplication, which is division.

Divide both sides by -3:

$$\frac{6}{-3} = \frac{-3z}{-3}$$

Simplify:

$$-2 = z$$

So, the solution to the equation is $z = -2$.

When we substitute the value of $z = -2$ back into the original equation, $6 = -3(-2)$, it simplifies to $6 = 6$. This confirms that our solution is correct because it satisfies the original equation.

One-Step Equations

Solve for the variable.

1. $6 + (x \div 6) = 7.3$

2. $16 = x + 8$

3. $1(3 - k) = -6$

4. $53 = x \times 6 + 5$

5. $m + 1 = 2$

6. $8s + s = 90$

7. $10 = z + (9 \div z)$

8. $10.5 = (s \div 6) + s$

9. $6 = 1 \times x + 3$

10. $69 = 10 \times m + 9$

11. $4 = 5a - 1$

12. $8 + 5y = 48$

13. $5 = 3 \times m + 2$

14. $6 = 3 \times (s - 5)$

15. $11 = y + (10 \div y)$

16. $2 = 3z - z$

17. $48 = (x \times 5) + x$

18. $3 \times x + 6 = 24$

19. $9 = 3(10 - z)$

20. $26 = z \times 9 - 1$

21. $2 + 7b = 58$

22. $11 = (m \times 10) + m$

23. $z \times 4 + z = 25$

24. $42 = x \times 8 + 2$

25. $a \times (8 - a) = 15$

26. $5 = s + (4 \div s)$

27. $2 \times k + 6 = 20$

28. $2 \times x + x = 3$

29. $8 + (s \div 6) = 9.3$

30. $24 = s \times (10 - s)$

31. $m \times 2 + 3 = 19$

32. $3 + z = 12$

33. $5 = 5(9 - k)$

34. $1 + (x \div 6) = 1.7$

35. $(6 \times b) + 4 = 58$

36. $s \times 9 + 2 = 65$

37. $28 = 4 + 6a$

38. $1.1 = (y \div 9) + y$

39. $7.7 = b + (10 \div b)$

40. $8(2 - k) = \text{-}8$

41. $6.6 = 6 + (z \div 10)$

42. $1.5 = m \div 6$

43. $k \times 7 = 21$

44. $9 + (s - 9) = 2$

45. $12 = 2 \times b$

46. $64 = y + (y \times 7)$

47. $9a + 8 = 71$

48. $6 = b + (8 \div b)$

Solving Two-Step Equations

Solving two-step equations involves finding the value of the variable that makes the equation true. In a two-step equation, two operations (addition, subtraction, multiplication, or division) are performed on the variable.

The goal is to isolate the variable on one side of the equation by performing inverse operations in the reverse order of operations.

For example:

Given the equation $18 = (10 + b) - 2$, where we want to solve for b.

To solve for b, we need to undo the operations that have been performed on b.

    1. Undo the subtraction by adding 2 to both sides:

$$18 + 2 = (10 + b) - 2 + 2$$
$$20 = 10 + b$$

    2. Undo the addition by subtracting 10 from both sides:

$$20 - 10 = 10 + b - 10$$
$$10 = b$$

So, the solution to the equation is $b = 10$

Let's substitute $b = 10$ back into the original equation to verify if it satisfies the equation:

Original equation:

$$18 = (10 + b) - 2:$$

Substitute $b = 10$:

$$18 = (10 + 10) - 2$$

simplify:

$$18 = 20 - 2$$
$$18 = 18$$

Since the equation simplifies to 18 =1 8, it confirms that our solution $b = 10$ is correct.

Two-Step Equations

Solve for the variable.

1. $6x + 6x - 6 = 30$

2. $6x + x - 9 = 26$

3. $40 = 10 \times (10 - x)$

4. $14 = 6 + (4 \times z)$

5. $110 = (3 + x) \times 10$

6. $9 \times b + 10 = 19$

7. $48 = 6a + 4a - 2$

8. $10y - 8 + 4y = 76$

9. $y + 6y + 6y = 104$

10. $28 = 3s - 5 + 8s$

11. $10b - 9 + 7b = 127$

12. $5m - 9 + 5m = 71$

13. $6m + 3 = 27$

14. $75 = y + 5 + 6y$

15. $5a - 7 + a = 41$

16. $1 = 5 \times m - 9$

17. $78 = 4x + x + 8x$

18. $80 = 8 \times (8 + z)$

19. $68 = 4a + 3a - 2$

20. $(8 - k) \times 8 = 16$

21. $a + 10 + 4a = 25$

22. $125 = 5b + 6 + (9b - 7)$

23. $72 = 7m + 8m + 9m$

24. $29 = 5y + 9$

25. $10 + (3m + 3) = 40$

26. $30 = 9 + (6k + 9)$

27. $10b - 10 + 7b = 126$

28. $9 = s + 2$

29. $2 \times (3 - y) = -14$

30. $8a + 8 = 24$

31. $3 + (7x + 7) = 52$

32. $-6 = m^1 + m - 8$

33. $10a + a + 9a = 160$

34. $81 = 3y + 6y$

35. $10a + 4a = 14$

36. $6 - (7 \times k) = -8$

37. $y + 5 + (7y - 9) = 12$

38. $9x + 1 = 82$

39. $5 \times (2 + z) = 40$

40. $78 = 10 \times z - 2$

41. $53 = s + 6s - 3$

42. $88 = 7 + (9 \times b)$

43. $23 = 3 + (y + 10)$

44. $(7x)^1 = 63$

45. $5z + z = 42$

46. $75 = (9 \times z) + 3$

47. $19 = 6y + 7$

48. $88 = 8x + 8$

Equations (Two Sides)

A two-sided equation is an equation where both sides have expressions with variables and constants. The goal when solving a two-sided equation is to find the value of the variable that makes both sides equal.

For example: Let's solve an equation:

$$9 + 8x + 8 = 64 + x + 2$$

- Combine Like Terms: Simplify each side of the equation by combining like terms (terms with the same variable or constants).

$$9 + 8x + 8 = 64 + x + 2$$
$$17 + 8x = 66 + x$$

- Isolate the Variable: Use inverse operations to isolate the variable on one side of the equation.

subtract x from both sides:
$$17 + 8x - x = 66 + x - x$$
$$17 + 7x = 66$$

subtracting 17 from both sides:
$$17 - 17 + 7x = 66 - 17$$
$$7x = 49$$

divide both sides by 7:
$$\frac{7x}{7} = \frac{49}{7} = x = 7$$

- Check Solution: Once you find the solution, substitute it back into the original equation to ensure it makes the equation true.

Substitute $x = 7$ back into the original equation:
$$9 + 8(7) + 8 = 64 + 7 + 2$$
$$9 + 56 + 8 = 64 + 7 + 2$$
$$73 = 73$$

Equations (Two Sides)

Solve for the variable.

1. $-18 + m = -2m$

2. $-9z = 50 + z$

3. $10x + -6 = 8x + -20$

4. $9z + 1 = -6 - -2z$

5. $2 - z = -2z + -2$

6. $10k + 2 = -160 - 8k$

7. $0 + -3b = -2b + 9$

8. $-36 + x + 10 = 4 + 5x + 2$

9. $9m = 64 + m$

10. $5 + 2s = 4 + s$

11. $27 + k = -5 + -5k + 8$

12. $-5 + -4b + 8 = 44 - b + -14$

13. $52 - b = 8b + 7$

14. $20 + y = -8y + -7$

15. $3 + 2x + -8 = -13 + x$

16. $-2 + 2m + -1 = -27 - m$

17. $-6 + 9a = -62 - -2a$

18. $-6 + m + 2 = 1 + -2m + -8$

19. $-14 - b = 4 + -7b$

20. $0 + m = -6 + 3m$

21. $1 + 10z = -71 + 2z$

22. $-3 + 8s + -5 = 29 + s + -9$

23. $10 - a = -8 + 2a$

24. $6z = 7 - z$

25. $7 + 4k = -33 - k$

26. $8 - a = 1 + -4a + -8$

27. $3 + 7b + 2 = 24 + b + -1$

28. $-3y + 2 = 58 - -4y$

29. $3 + 2x + 1 = 13 - x + 6$

30. $4y + -4 = -24 - y$

31. $-1 + 9a + 3 = 66 + a$

32. $-56 - s = -8s$

33. $1 + m = 2m + -2$

34. $2z = -6 + z$

35. $-10 + 7b = -127 - 6b$

36. $9x = 64 + x$

<u>**Simplifying Expressions**</u>

It involves combining like terms and performing operations to make the expression easier to understand and work with.

Let's simplify the expression:

$$2x - 2x + 8 + 4$$

- **Combine like terms: First, we look for terms with the same variable and exponent. In this expression, $2x$ and $-2x$ are like terms, so they can be combined:**

$$2x - 2x = 0$$

- **Substitute the simplified terms: After combining the like terms, the expression becomes:**

$$0 + 8 + 4$$

- **Combine the remaining terms: Now, we add the constants together:**

$$8 + 4 = 12$$

Simplify Expressions

1. $10z - 8z + 6 + 16$

2. $-12m - 16 - 2m$

3. $8x + 1 + x$

4. $m + 13 + 17m$

5. $17 - 18(19x - 17)$

6. $20z + 18 - 7z + 6 + 20z + 1$

7. $-19m - 18 + 7 - 2m$

8. $m + 11 + 9m$

9. $18z + 6 - 20 - 10z + z$

10. $17 + y - 15y$

11. $10 + 2(10k - 15)$

12. $18 - 15(20z - 10)$

13. $-17x + 1 + 17x$

14. $-11 + 6y - 5y - 2 - 16y$

15. $1 + 3k - 9k$

16. $19 + 14k + 4 + 7k$

17. $19x - 18x + 19x - 11 + 11$

18. $-19k + 8 - 3 + 9k$

19. $7x - 7x + 2 + 13$

20. $18 + 4 + 10z - 4z + 1 - 12z$

21. $20 + 13 + 15k - k + 2 - 10k$

22. $2x + 12 - 14 - x + 7x$

23. $-19 + 2k - 6k - 13 + 18k$

24. $13 + 2(-13y + 20)$

25. $-k + k$

26. $17 + m - 5 + 15m$

27. $4 - 18(12z - 7)$

28. $16m - 18 - 8m + 19 - 2$

29. $-6x - 8 - 7 - 15x$

30. $14m + 14 - 4m - 16 + 7m - 9$

31. $11m - 4 + 16m - 11 + m + 6$

32. $9x + 20 + 18x$

33. $11 + 3k - k + 16 - 15k$

34. $m + m$

35. $10 + 14 + 20k - 14k + 12 - 10k$

36. $6m - 5m + 16m - 1 + 19$

37. $y + 9 + y$

38. $12 + 4(k - 18)$

39. $-2m - 10 - 6 - 19m$

40. $-18m - m$

41. $20 - 14(y - 3)$

42. $m - 16 + 11m - 20 + 10m + 4$

43. $x + 3 + x$

44. $m + 17m$

45. $19m - m$

46. $14y + 15 + y$

47. $9y - 15y + 7 + 18$

48. $-x + 4x$

49. $-10m + 16m + 15 - 7m$

50. $-7 + 10z - 17z - 18 - 18z$

51. $20k + 10 - 13k + 15 + 17k + 14$

52. $3 - 20k + 14 - 8k + 20 - 4k$

53. $-10 - 5y + 10 - 5y$

54. $-17k + 10 - 12k$

55. $z + 14 - 10z - 15 + 9z - 14$

56. $-20 + 1 - x + 15x - 1 + 5x$

57. $16m - 19m + 13m - 16 + 9$

58. $-18y + 15 + 16y$

59. $-11k + 2k$

60. $-5 - 15m + 2m - 15 + 11m$

61. $2k + 15 - k + 7 + 20k + 14$

62. $6 + 7 + 14z - 20z + 10 - 9z$

63. $-y + 13 + 7y + 4 + 8y - 1$

64. $15 + 5(-4x + 20)$

<u>**Evaluating Equations**</u>

Evaluating expressions involves substituting given values for variables in an expression and then performing the indicated operations to find the result.

For example: Let's evaluate $4x - 10$, when $x = 3$:

Step 1: Substitute the given value for the variable:

Replace every occurrence of x in the expression $4x - 10$ with the given value, which is 3:

$$= 4(3) - 10$$

Step 2: Perform the operations:

Perform the indicated operations according to the order of operations (PEMDAS - Parentheses, Exponents, Multiplication and Division, Addition and Subtraction):

$$= 4 \times 3 - 10$$

Step 3: Simplify:

Calculate the result:

$$12 - 10 = 2$$

NAME: ___________

Evaluating Equations

Simplify the following equations when the value of $n = 2$

1. $-5n + n =$

2. $(-6n)^1 =$

3. $2 \times (-10 + n) =$

4. $-1 \times n + n =$

5. $-1n + (-1)n =$

6. $-1n^2 + n^2 =$

7. $6 \times n + n =$

8. $1 + 4n - (-10 + n) =$

Evaluating Equations

Simplify the following equations when the value of n = -10

1. $3 \times (n - 4) =$

2. $-6 + n(7 - n) + 0n =$

3. $n + (-3 \div n) =$

4. $n + (1 \div n) =$

5. $(-1 - n) \times (-4) =$

6. $(0 - n) \times (-5n + 4) =$

7. $n \times (0 - n) =$

8. $4 \times n - 10 =$

Evaluating Equations

Simplify the following equations when the value of n = 4

1. $(-9 \times n) + (-6)n - 8 =$

2. $-7(n + (-7)) + (-3)n =$

3. $-2(n - 2) + (-7)n =$

4. $(-5 + n) \times 1 =$

5. $9 + 6n - (3 + n) =$

6. $9 \times (n - (-8)) =$

7. $(8n + (-8))(-1n + (-9)) =$

8. $-1(n - (-4)) + 5n =$

Evaluating Equations

Simplify the following equations when the value of n = 5

1. $-10n + n =$

2. $(-1 \div n) + 6 =$

3. $-5 \times n + (-1) =$

4. $(-2n + (-5)) + (9n + (-9)) =$

5. $3(1 + n) =$

6. $(-5 - n) \times (-8) =$

7. $-10n + (-10) \times (n + (-10)) - 5 =$

8. $(0n + 9)(-8n - (-4)) =$

Evaluating Equations

Simplify the following equations when the value of $n = -5$

1. $(9 + n) \times (-2) =$

2. $n + (-1 \div n) =$

3. $5 + n(9 - n) + (-3)n =$

4. $n^1 + n - 7 =$

5. $3 + (n - 4)(0n) =$

6. $7^3 + n^1 =$

7. $0 \times (-10 + n) =$

8. $6n + 6n - (-1) =$

Evaluating Equations

Simplify the following equations when the value of n = -1

1. $-2 + (-9n + (-10)) - 6 + (3n) =$

2. $n \times (-2) - 3 =$

3. $n^3 + n - 1 =$

4. $(5 + n)(4n - (-8)) =$

5. $n + (n \times 7) =$

6. $-2 \times n =$

7. $(-8 \times n) + 4n - (-6) =$

8. $(-9n + 6) \times (n - (-1)) =$

Evaluating Equations

Simplify the following equations when the value of $n = -8$

1. $n \times 0 + n =$

2. $(10n + 6)(2n + 6) =$

3. $(-6 + n) \times 1 =$

4. $(-5 \times n) - 6 =$

5. $8 + (-9n + (-9)) - (-6) + (10n) =$

6. $-5 + (-9)n =$

7. $3 + (3n - n)(2 + n) =$

8. $(-9n + 7)(4n + (-5)) =$

Evaluating Equations

Simplify the following equations when the value of $n = 3$

1. $n + (n \times 2) =$

2. $n \times 1 + (-10) =$

3. $5 \times n + n =$

4. $8 + n(1 - n) + (-10)n =$

5. $(-6n + 2)(-2n - (-2)) =$

6. $n^1 + n - (-6) =$

7. $5n - n =$

8. $-3(n + (-8)) + n(6 - n) =$

Plot Lines

To plot the lines using the given points, we'll first locate each point on the coordinate plane, and then connect the points to form the lines. Let's plot each line one by one:

$$A = (-6, -3) \qquad B = (0, 3)$$

$$C = (-4, -1) \qquad D = (1, 4)$$

$$E = (4, 7) \qquad F = (2, 5)$$

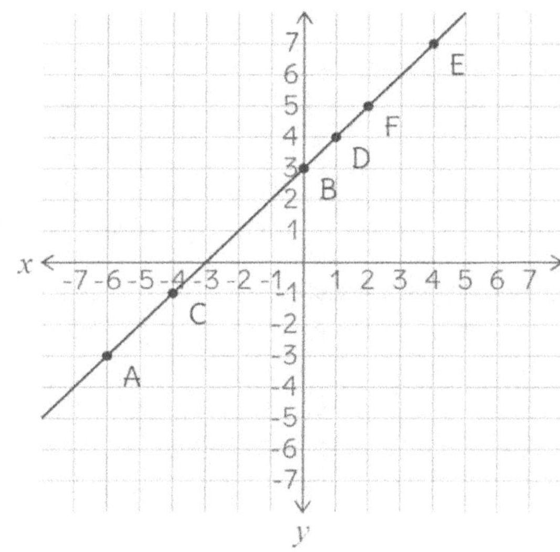

Plotting Lines

Plot and draw the lines.

1.

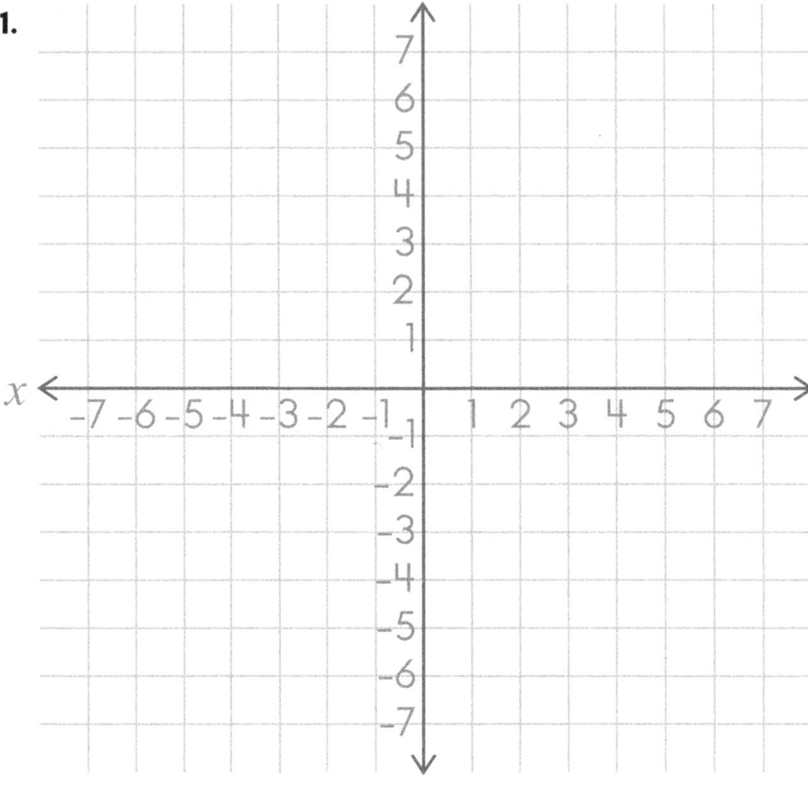

A = (6, 0)   B = (2, 2)

C = (-6, 6)   D = (0, 3)

E = (4, 1)   F = (-4, 5)

2.

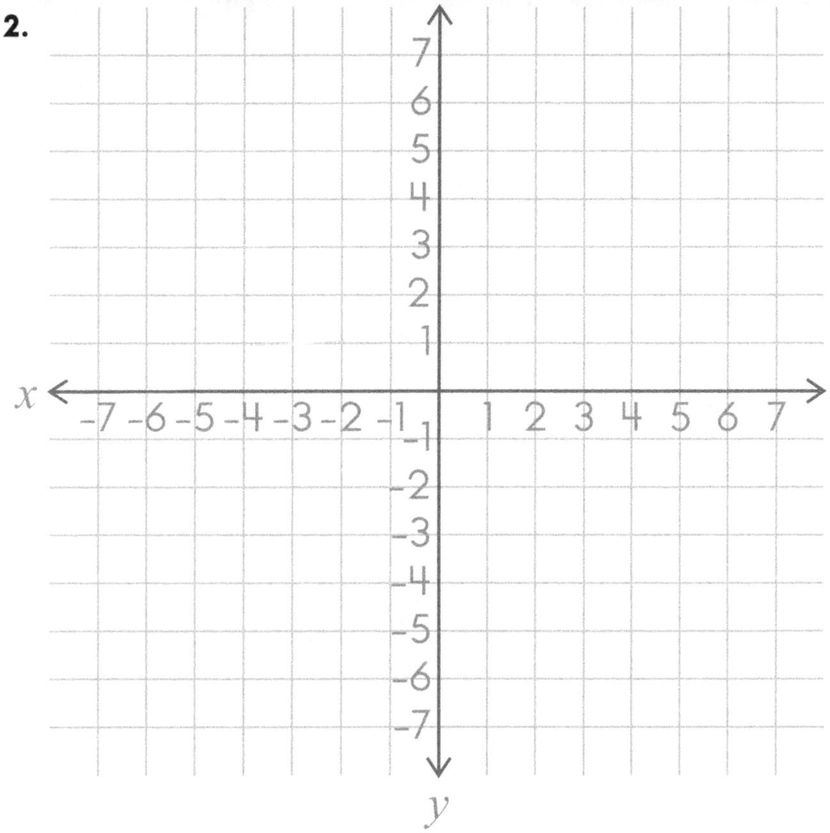

A = (-1, 4)   B = (1, 2)

C = (4, -1)   D = (2, 1)

E = (5, -2)   F = (0, 3)

3.

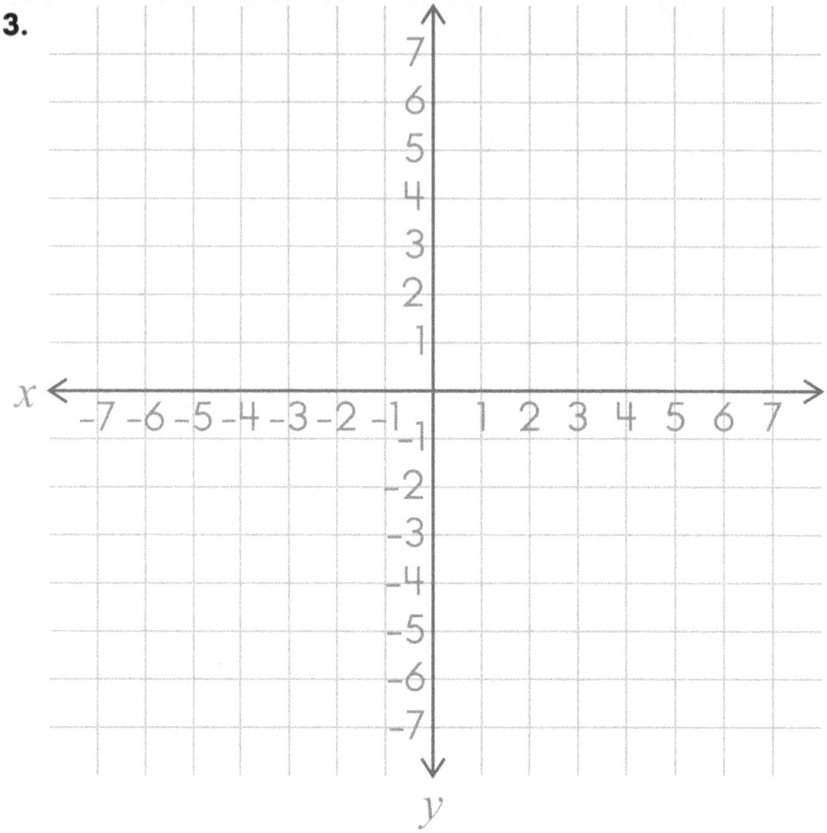

A = (-4, 3)   B = (0, -1)

C = (4, -5)   D = (3, -4)

E = (-5, 4)   F = (-3, 2)

4.

A = (5, 4)   B = (2, -2)

C = (0, -6)   D = (6, 6)

E = (4, 2)   F = (1, -4)

5.

A = (3, 1)   B = (1, 3)

C = (-3, 7)   D = (6, -2)

E = (-2, 6)   F = (5, -1)

Cartesian Coordinates

The Cartesian Coordinate System, also known as the x-y plane, provides a method for representing points on a graph using two perpendicular lines: the x-axis and the y-axis. At their intersection, denoted by the letter "O", lies the origin.

To plot a point on this system, we use coordinates, consisting of two numbers. The first number represents the horizontal movement from the origin (x-coordinate), while the second number represents the vertical movement (y-coordinate). These coordinates are written as an ordered pair (x, y).

For instance, let's plot these coordinates:

$$A = (1, 3) \qquad B = (5, 0) \qquad C = (8, 6)$$

$$D = (9, 5) \qquad E = (1, 9) \qquad F = (3, 1)$$

$$G = (0, 8) \qquad H = (4, 6) \qquad I = (4, 9)$$

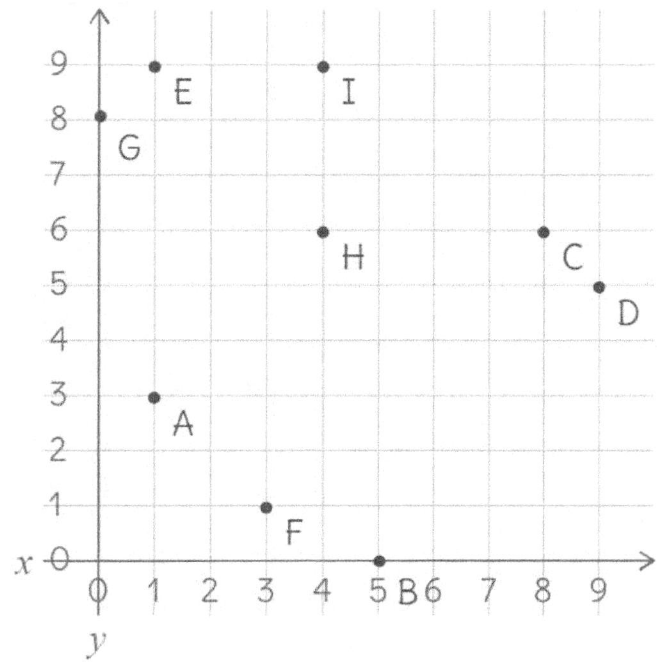

Cartesian Coordinates (Four Quadrants)

In a Cartesian coordinate system with four quadrants, there are two perpendicular number lines intersecting at the origin (0,0), dividing the plane into four quadrants.

To plot a point in this Cartesian coordinate system, we use an ordered pair (x, y), where x represents the distance from the y-axis, and y represents the distance from the x-axis.

For instance, let's plot these coordinates:

$$A = (-4, 1) \quad B = (2, 1) \quad C = (4, 2)$$

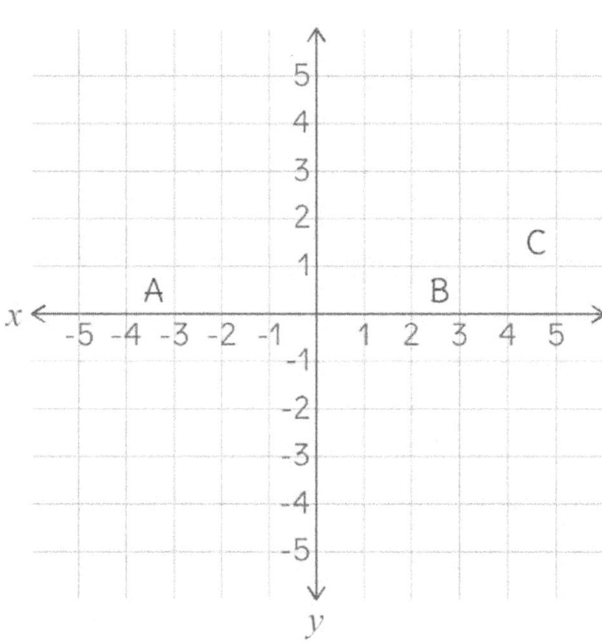

Cartesian Coordinates With Four Quadrants

Fill in as indicated.

1.

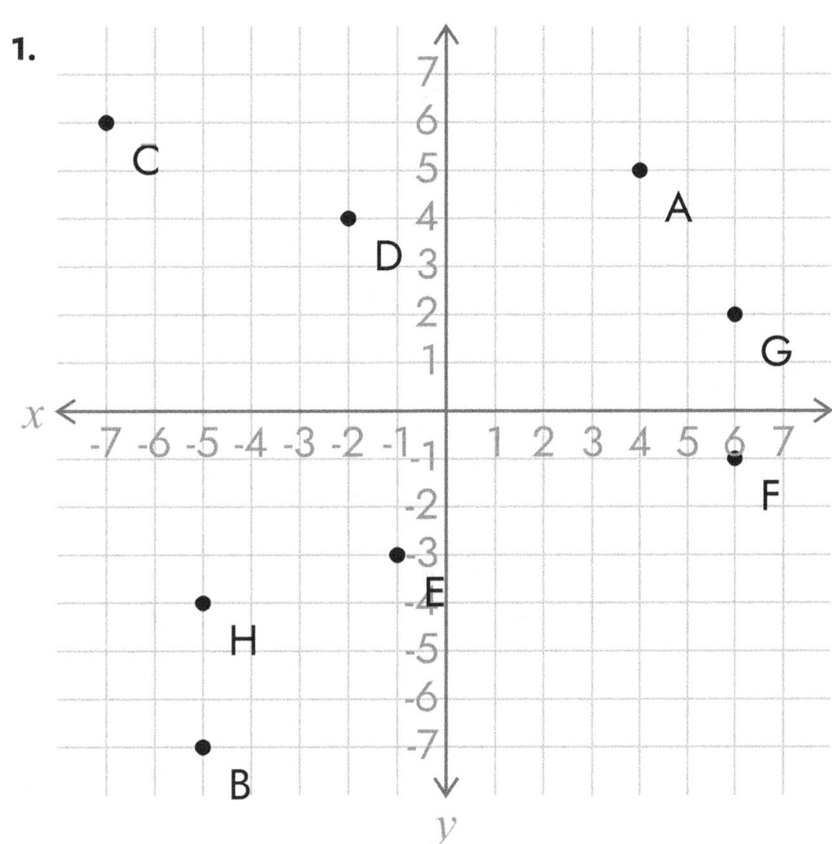

A = ______   B = ______   C = ______

D = ______   E = ______   F = ______

G = ______   H = ______

2.

A = _______   B = _______   C = _______

D = _______   E = _______   F = _______

G = _______   H = _______

3.

$$x, y$$

A = ________   B = ________   C = ________

D = ________   E = ________   F = ________

G = ________   H = ________

Linear Functions

A linear equation is an algebraic equation that represents a straight line when graphed on a coordinate plane. It consists of variables raised to the power of 1 (i.e., no exponents higher than 1) and constant coefficients.

The general form of a linear equation in one variable x is:

$$ax + b = 0$$

Where a and b are constants, and x is the variable.

Let's solve the linear equation:

$$-2x + 9 = 5$$

- Isolate the variable term: We want to isolate the term containing x on one side of the equation. To do this, we'll move the constant term to the other side. Subtract 9 from both sides:

$$-2x + 9 - 9 = 5 - 9$$

$$-2x = -4$$

- Divide by the coefficient of the variable: To solve for x, divide both sides by the coefficient of x, which is -2:

$$\frac{-2x}{-2} = \frac{-4}{-2}$$

$$x = 2$$

Linear Equations

Solve for the variable.

1) $-5y + (-2) = -37$

2) $-1(-2y - 2) = 12$

3) $-8y + 5 = -19$

4) $-7y + (-6)y - 2 = 115$

5) $-1x + (-7) = -7$

6) $5x + 0 = 40$

7) $4y = -12$

8) $6y + (-1)y - (-1) = 46$

9) $10x = -80$

10) $9(8y - (-3)) = 99$

11) $-3(8y - 2) = -162$

12) $7x = -56$

13) $10y + (-9)y = -7$

14) $-6y + (-6)y = 60$

15) $-8x = 8$

16) $3x = 18$

17) $10(-6x - (-6)) = 360$

18) $x + 3 = 10$

19) $9y + 0y - 10 = -91$

20) $10x + 0 = 50$

21) $-6y + (-7) = -37$

22) $7x + (-3)x - 5 = 11$

23) $8(3x - 5) = -256$

24) $4(-2y - (-9)) = 36$

<u>**Slop from Two Points**</u>

The slope between two points on a Cartesian coordinate system is a measure of the steepness of the line connecting those points. It's calculated by finding the change in the y-coordinates divided by the change in the x-coordinates.

- The coordinates of the first point as $(x1 , y1) = (2,-30)$.

- The coordinates of the second point as $(x2 , y2) = (-5,40)$.

The formula to calculate the slope (m) between two points:

$$\frac{y2 - y1}{x2 - x1}$$

Find Slope from two Points

1) (-17, -1) and (-12 , 12)

2) (5, -2) and (13 , 11)

3) (11, -12) and (15 , -9)

4) (-10, 15) and (-2 , 18)

5) (9, -5) and (-14 , -12)

6) (-17, -11) and (-11 , 18)

7) (10, -4) and (-6 , -17)

8) (-5, 18) and (-15 , 6)

9) (12, 11) and (-3 , 3)

10) (18, 4) and (-18 , -8)

11) (-11, -10) and (17 , -14)

12) (-14, -13) and (0 , -2)

13) (-12, -2) and (13 , 18)

14) (-13, -19) and (9 , 14)

15) (-11, -10) and (-18 , -12)

16) (-17, 9) and (-5 , 13)

17) (-17, -11) and (0 , 0)

18) (-2, 15) and (20 , -15)

19) (-8, 15) and (19 , 14)

20) (-8, -18) and (12 , 2)

21) (16, 17) and (15 , 18)

22) (-15, -13) and (-2 , 11)

23) (-19, 3) and (-6 , 7)

24) (2, 14) and (-12 , 0)

Graphing Linear Equation

Graphing a linear equation involves plotting the points that satisfy the equation on a coordinate plane and connecting them to form a straight line. Linear equations are equations of the form $y = mx + b$, where m represents the slope of the line, and b represents the y-intercept, the point where the line intersects the y-axis.

To graph a linear equation:

1. Identify the slope (m) and y-intercept (b) from the equation.

2. Plot the y-intercept $(0,b))$ as a point on the y-axis.

3. Use the slope to find additional points on the line. The slope represents the change in y for every unit change in x.

4. Connect the points to form a straight line.

For example, to graph the equation:

$$y = \frac{9}{4}x - 8$$

1. **Identify the slope and y-intercept:** The slope is $\frac{9}{4}$, and the y-intercept is −8.

2. **Plot the y-intercept:** Plot the point $(0,-8)$.

3. **Use the slope to plot additional points:** the slop is $\frac{9}{4}$ to find another point. we will move up 9 units and 4 units to the right from the y-intercept to find another point.

4. **Draw the line:** Once we have at least two points, we can draw a straight line.

We can continue this process to plot more points and extend the line further if needed.

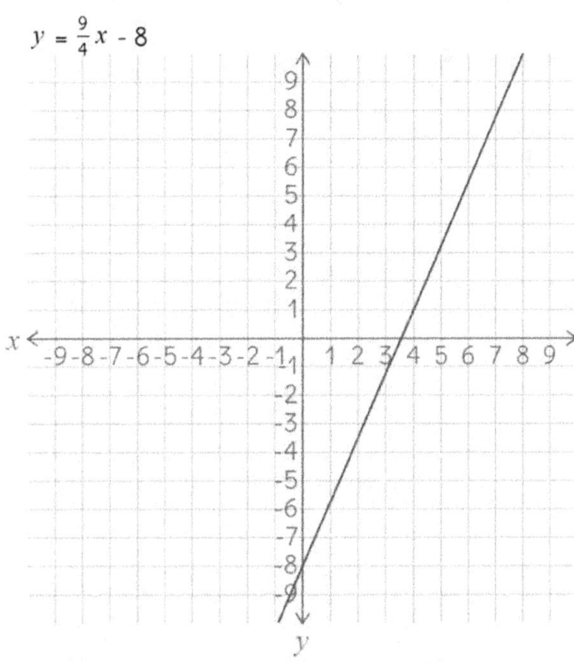

Graphing Linear Equations

1) $y = \dfrac{3}{4}x - 1$

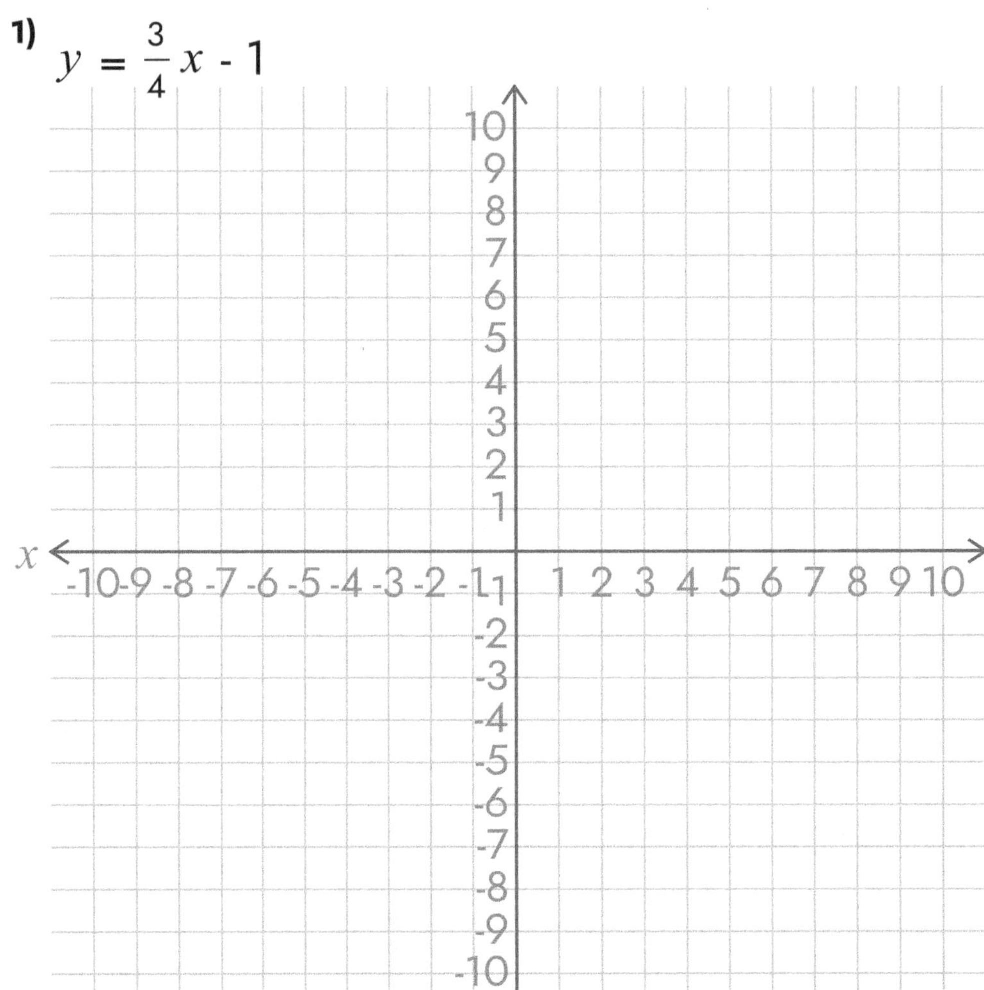

2) $y = \dfrac{5}{4}x - 1$

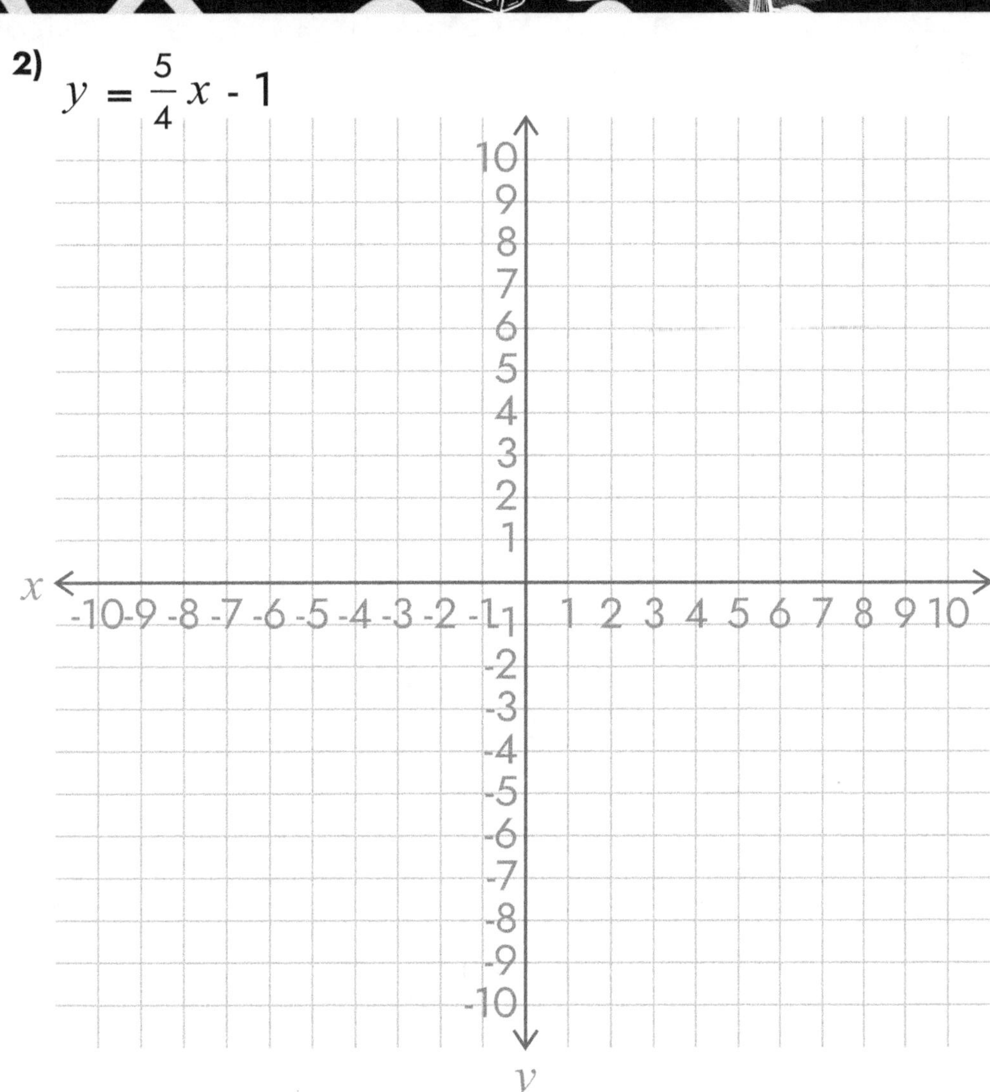

3) $x = -6$

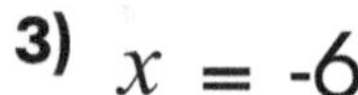

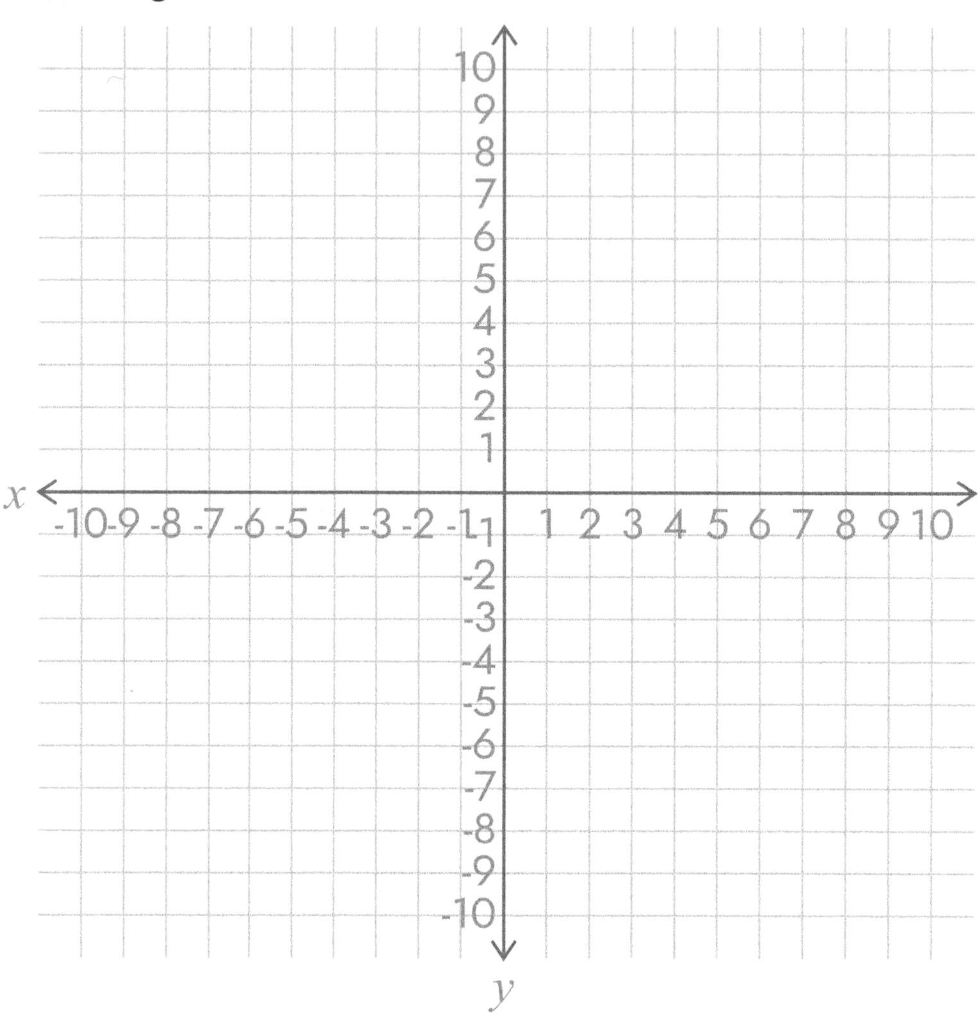

4) $x = 8$

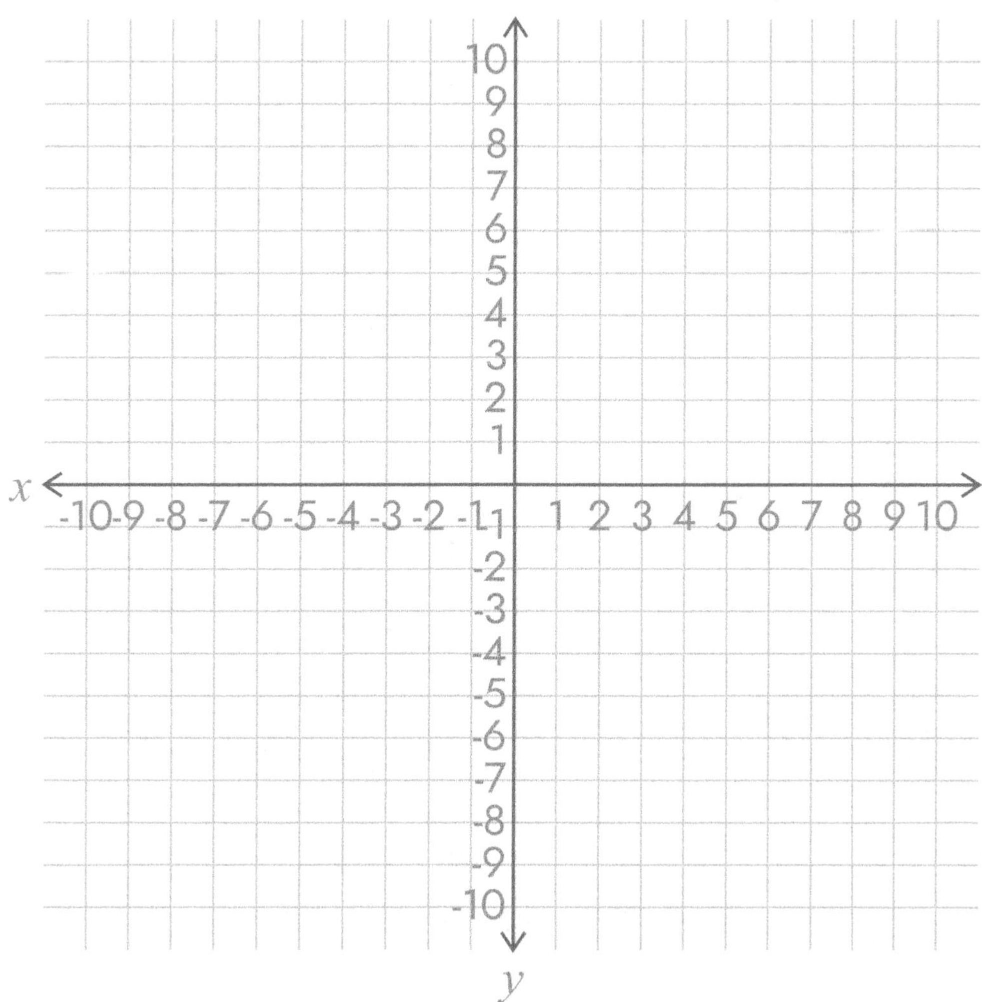

5) $y = \dfrac{5}{2}x + 9$

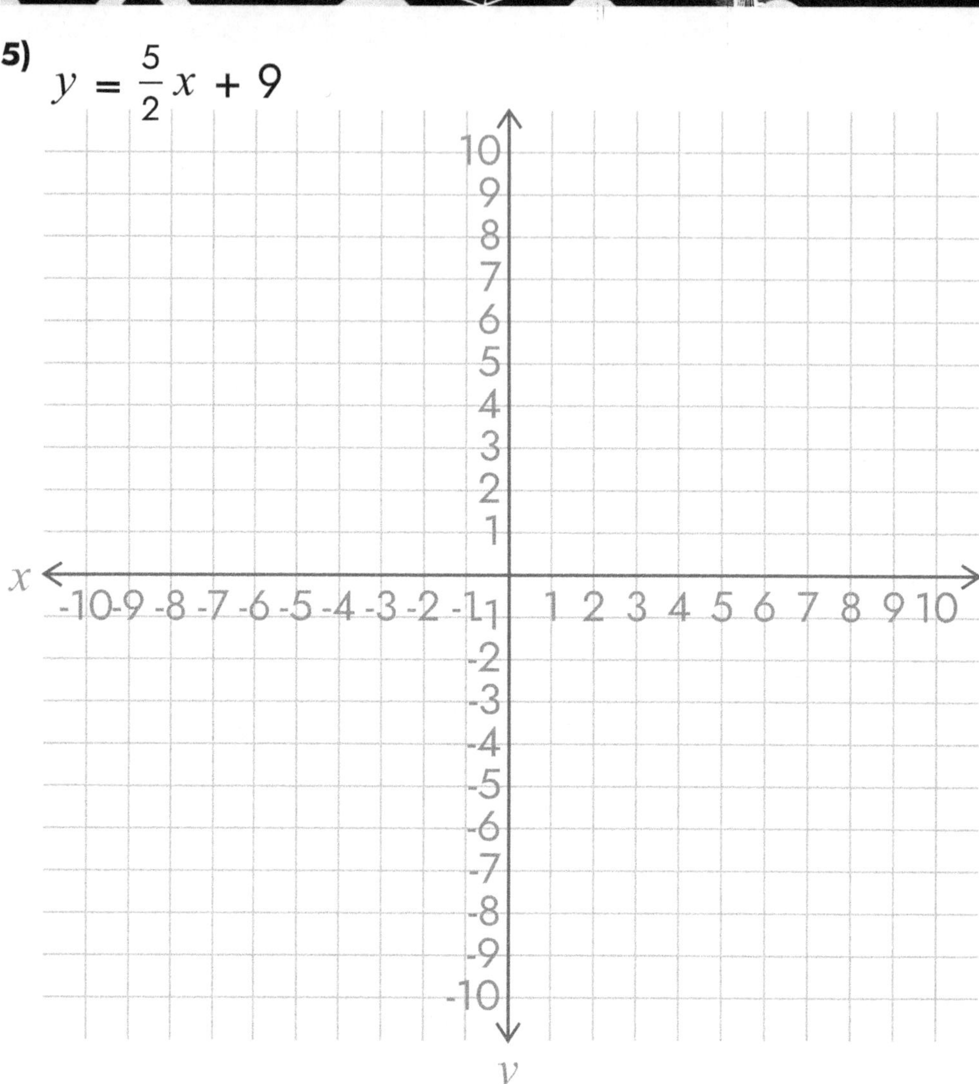

ANSWERS

Page 1:   Order of Operations

1. 10	**2.** 14	**3.** 25	**4.** 6,404	**5.** 14	**6.** 324	**7.** 14
8. 18	**9.** 144	**10.** 45	**11.** 11	**12.** 19	**13.** 40	**14.** 121
15. 13	**16.** 18	**17.** 70	**18.** 14	**19.** 7	**20.** 24	**21.** 4
22. 36	**23.** 15	**24.** 70	**25.** 425	**26.** -7	**27.** 79	**28.** 154
29. 64	**30.** 17	**31.** 120	**32.** 12	**33.** 66	**34.** 4	**35.** 52
36. 15	**37.** 20	**38.** 39	**39.** 130	**40.** 258	**41.** 47	**42.** 36
43. 109	**44.** 19	**45.** 557	**46.** 15	**47.** 44	**48.** 143	

Page 6:   One-Step Equations

1. 8	**2.** 8	**3.** 9	**4.** 8	**5.** 1	**6.** 10
7. 9 or 1	**8.** 9	**9.** 3	**10.** 6	**11.** 1	**12.** 8
13. 1	**14.** 7	**15.** 10 or 1	**16.** 1	**17.** 8	**18.** 6
19. 7	**20.** 3	**21.** 8	**22.** 1	**23.** 5	**24.** 5
25. 5 or 3	**26.** 4 or 1	**27.** 7	**28.** 1	**29.** 8	**30.** 6 or 4
31. 8	**32.** 9	**33.** 8	**34.** 4	**35.** 9	**36.** 7
37. 4	**38.** 1	**39.** 6	**40.** 3	**41.** 6	**42.** 9
43. 3	**44.** 2	**45.** 6	**46.** 8	**47.** 7	**48.** 4 or 2

Page 12:   Two-Step Equations

1. 3	**2.** 5	**3.** 6	**4.** 2	**5.** 8	**6.** 1	**7.** 5	**8.** 6	**9.** 8
10. 3	**11.** 8	**12.** 8	**13.** 4	**14.** 10	**15.** 8	**16.** 2	**17.** 6	**18.** 2

19. 10   **20.** 6   **21.** 3   **22.** 9   **23.** 3   **24.** 4   **25.** 9   **26.** 2   **27.** 8

28. 7   **29.** 10   **30.** 2   **31.** 6   **32.** 1   **33.** 8   **34.** 9   **35.** 1   **36.** 2

37. 2   **38.** 9   **39.** 6   **40.** 8   **41.** 8   **42.** 9   **43.** 10   **44.** 9   **45.** 7

46. 8   **47.** 2   **48.** 10

Page 18:   Equations (Two Sides)

1. $m = 6$ **2.** $z = -5$ **3.** $x = -7$ **4.** $z = -1$ **5.** $z = -4$ **6.** $k = -9$

7. $b = -9$ **8.** $x = -8$ **9.** $m = 8$ **10.** $s = -1$ **11.** $k = -4$ **12.** $b = -9$

13. $b = 5$ **14.** $y = -3$ **15.** $x = -8$ **16.** $m = -8$ **17.** $a = -8$ **18.** $m = -1$

19. $b = 3$ **20.** $m = 3$ **21.** $z = -9$ **22.** $s = 4$ **23.** $a = 6$ **24.** $z = 1$

25. $k = -8$ **26.** $a = -5$ **27.** $b = 3$ **28.** $y = -8$ **29.** $x = 5$ **30.** $y = -4$

31. $a = 8$ **32.** $s = 8$ **33.** $m = 3$ **34.** $z = -6$ **35.** $b = -9$ **36.** $x = 8$

Page 27:   Simplify Expressions

1. $2z + 22$ **2.** $-14m - 16$ **3.** $9x + 1$ **4.** $18m + 13$

5. $-342x + 323$ **6.** $33z + 25$ **7.** $-21m - 11$ **8.** $10m + 11$

9. $9z - 14$ **10.** $-14y + 17$ **11.** $20k - 20$ **12.** $-300z + 168$

13. 1   **14.** $-15y - 13$ **15.** $-6k + 1$ **16.** $21k + 23$

17. $20x$ **18.** $-10k + 5$ **19.** 15   **20.** $-6z + 23$

21. $4k + 35$ **22.** $8x - 2$ **23.** $14k - 32$ **24.** $-26y + 53$

25. 0   **26.** $16m + 12$ **27.** $-216z + 130$ **28.** $8m - 1$

29. $-21x - 15$ **30.** $17m - 11$ **31.** $28m - 9$ **32.** $27x + 20$

33. $-13k + 27$ **34.** $2m$ **35.** $-4k + 36$ **36.** $17m + 18$

37. $2y + 9$ **38.** $4k - 60$ **39.** $-21m - 16$ **40.** $-19m$

41. −14y + 62 **42.** 22m − 32 **43.** 2x + 3 **44.** 18m

45. 18m **46.** 15y + 15 **47.** −6y + 25 **48.** 3x

49. −m + 15 **50.** −25z − 25 **51.** 24k + 39 **52.** −32k + 37

53. −10y **54.** −29k + 10 **55.** -15 **56.** 19x − 20

57. 10m − 7 **58.** −2y + 15 **59.** −9k **60.** −2m − 20

61. 21k + 36 **62.** −15z + 23 **63.** 14y + 16 **64.** −20x + 115

Page 35: Evaluating Equations

1. -8 **2.** -12 **3.** -16 **4.** 0 **5.** -4 **6.** 0 **7.** 14 **8.** 17

Page 36: Evaluating Equations

1. -42 **2.** -176 **3.** -9.7 **4.** -10.1 **5.** -36 **6.** 540 **7.** -100 **8.** -50

Page 37: Evaluating Equations

1. -68 **2.** 9 **3.** -32 **4.** -1 **5.** 26 **6.** 108 **7.** -312 **8.** 12

Page 38: Evaluating Equations

1. -45 **2.** 5.8 **3.** -26 **4.** 21 **5.** 18 **6.** 80 **7.** -5 **8.** -324

Page 39: Evaluating Equations

1. -8 **2.** -4.8 **3.** -50 **4.** -17 **5.** 3 **6.** 338 **7.** 0 **8.** -59

Page 40: Evaluating Equations

1. -12 **2.** -1 **3.** -3 **4.** 16 **5.** -8 **6.** 2 **7.** 10 **8.** 0

Page 41: Evaluating Equations

1. -8 **2.** 740 **3.** -14 **4.** 34 **5.** -3 **6.** 67 **7.** 99

8. -2,923

Page 42: Evaluating Equations

1. 9 **2.** -7 **3.** 18 **4.** -28 **5.** 64 **6.** 12 **7.** 12 **8.** 24

Page 43: Plotting Lines

1. 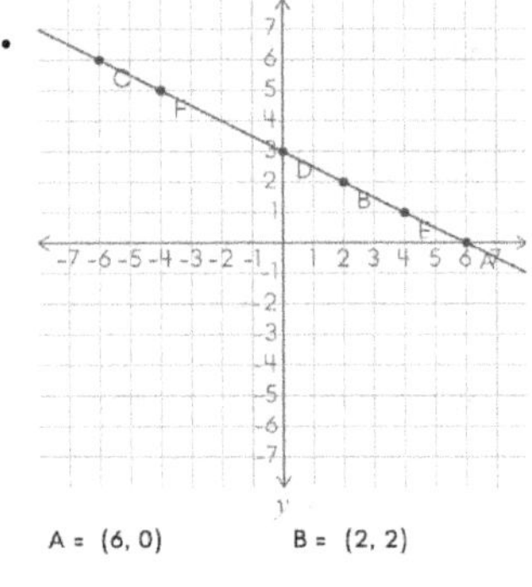

A = (6, 0)   B = (2, 2)

C = (-6, 6)   D = (0, 3)

E = (4, 1)   F = (-4, 5)

2. 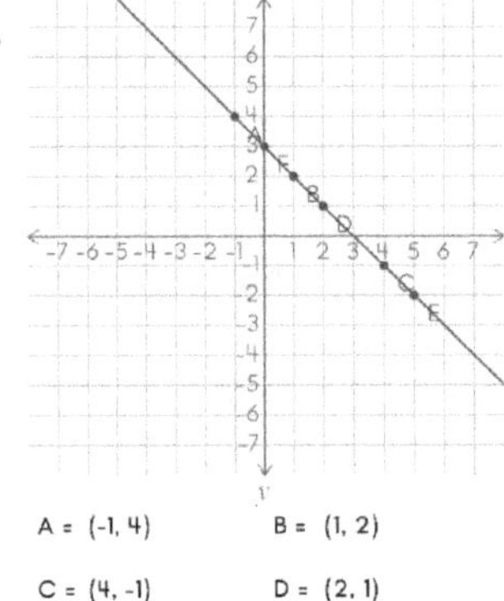

A = (-1, 4)   B = (1, 2)

C = (4, -1)   D = (2, 1)

E = (5, -2)   F = (0, 3)

3. 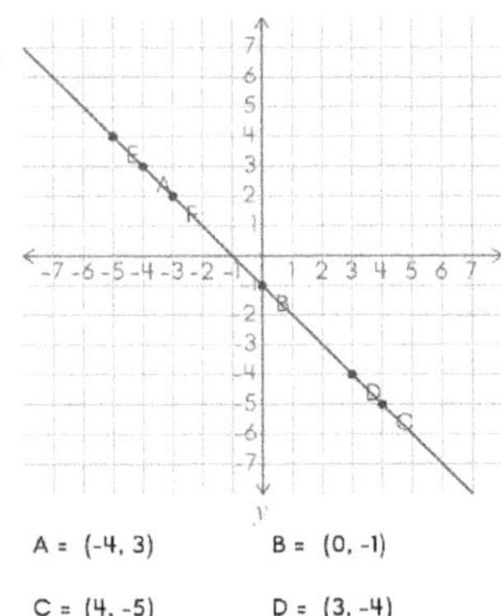

A = (-4, 3)   B = (0, -1)

C = (4, -5)   D = (3, -4)

E = (-5, 4)   F = (-3, 2)

4. 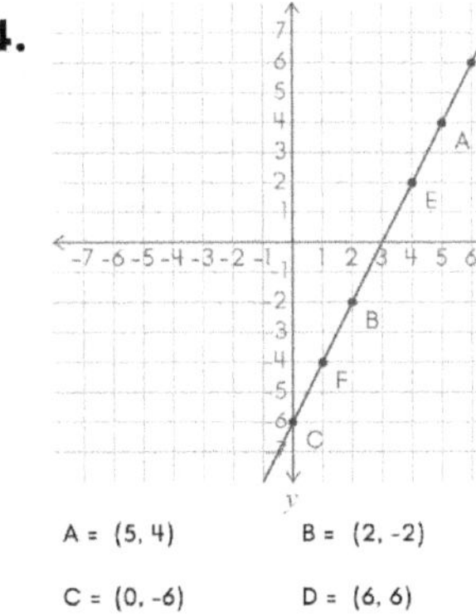

A = (5, 4)   B = (2, -2)

C = (0, -6)   D = (6, 6)

E = (4, 2)   F = (1, -4)

5. 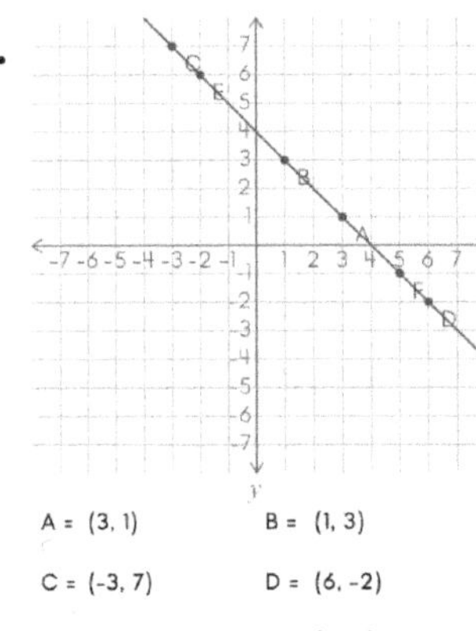

A = (3, 1)   B = (1, 3)

C = (-3, 7)   D = (6, -2)

E = (-2, 6)   F = (5, -1)

Page 48: Cartesian Coordinates With Four Quadrants

1. 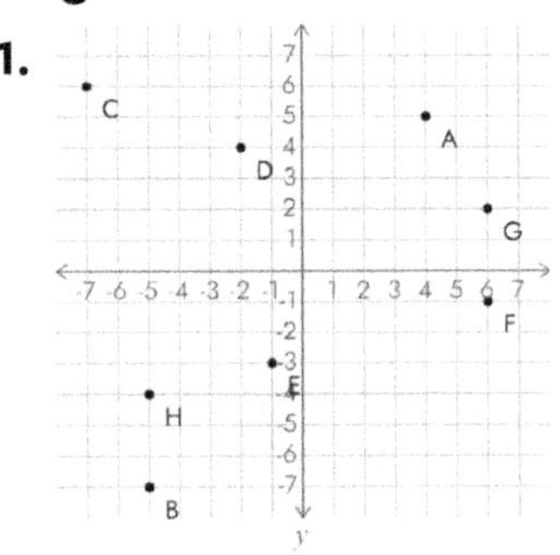

A = (4, 5)   B = (-5, -7)   C = (-7, 6)

D = (-2, 4)   E = (-1, -3)   F = (6, -1)

G = (6, 2)   H = (-5, -4)

2. 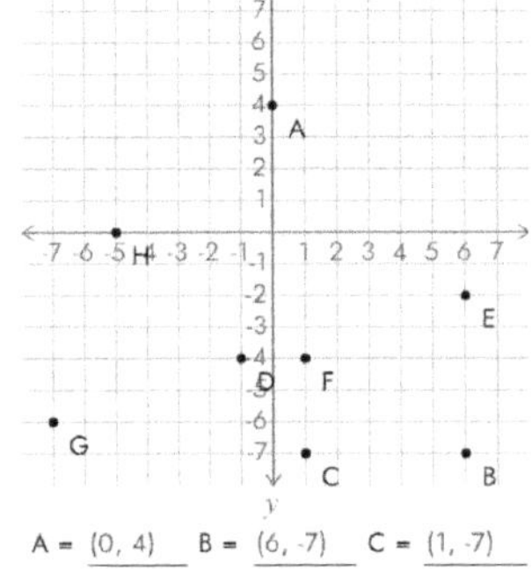

A = (0, 4)   B = (6, -7)   C = (1, -7)

D = (-1, -4)   E = (6, -2)   F = (1, -4)

G = (-7, -6)   H = (-5, 0)

3. 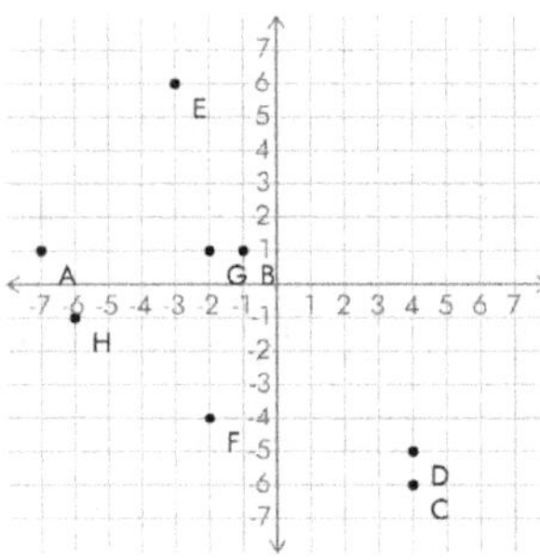

A = (-7, 1)   B = (-1, 1)   C = (4, -6)

D = (4, -5)   E = (-3, 6)   F = (-2, -4)

G = (-2, 1)   H = (-6, -1)

Page 51: Linear Equations

1. 7 **2.** 5 **3.** 3 **4.** -9 **5.** 0 **6.** 8 **7.** -3 **8.** 9 **9.** -8 **10.** 1

11. 7 **12.** -8 **13.** -7 **14.** -5 **15.** -1 **16.** 6 **17.** -5 **18.** 7 **19.** -9 **20.** 5

21. 5 **22.** 4 **23.** -9 **24.** 0

Page 54: Find Slope from two Points

1. 2.6 **2.** 1.62 **3.** 0.75 **4.** 0.38 **5.** 0.30 **6.** 4.83 **7.** 0.81

8. 1.2 **9.** 0.53 **10.** 0.33 **11.** -0.14 **12.** 0.79 **13.** 0.8 **14.** 1.5

15. 0.29 **16.** 0.33 **17.** 0.65 **18.** -1.36 **19.** -0.04 **20.** 1 **21.** -1

22. 1.85 **23.** 0.31 **24.** 1

Page 57: Graphing Linear Equations

1. 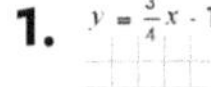

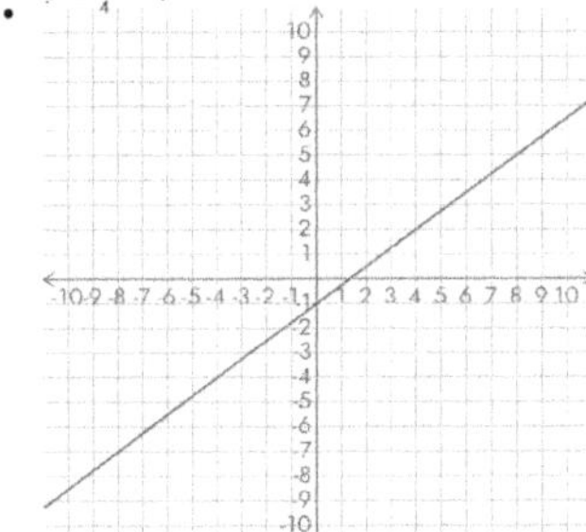

2. $y = \frac{5}{4}x - 1$
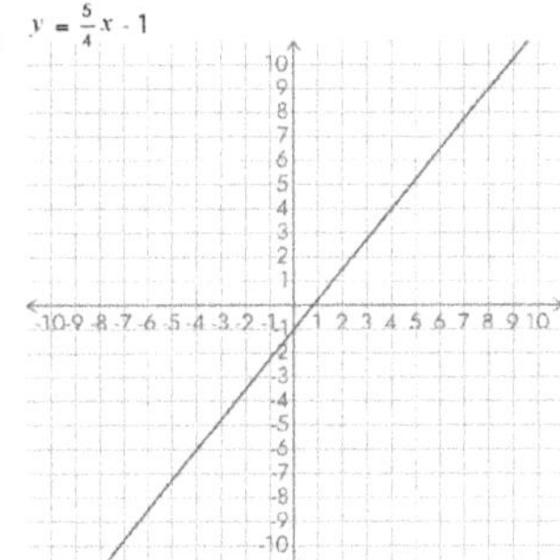

3. $x = -6$
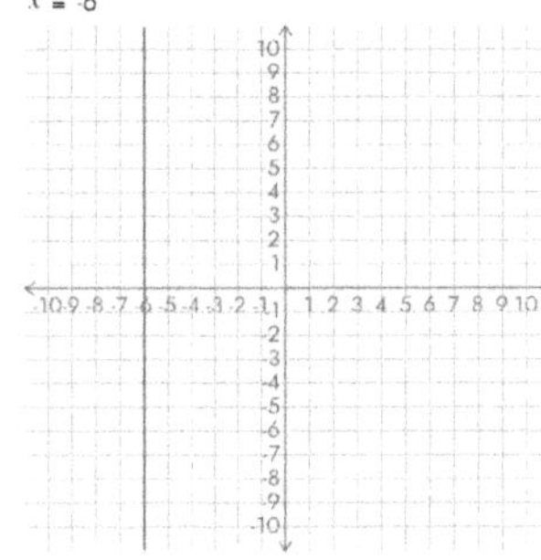

4. 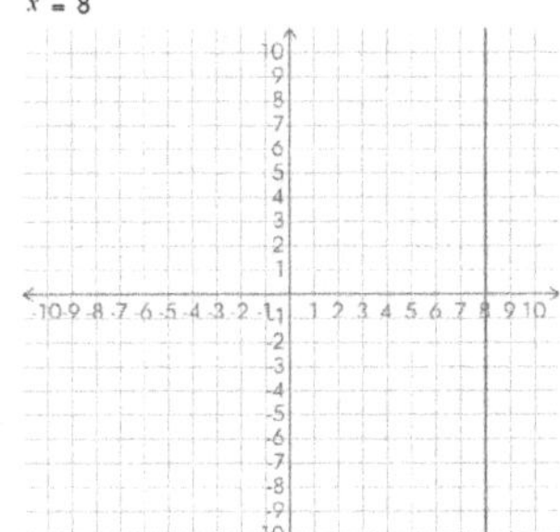

5. 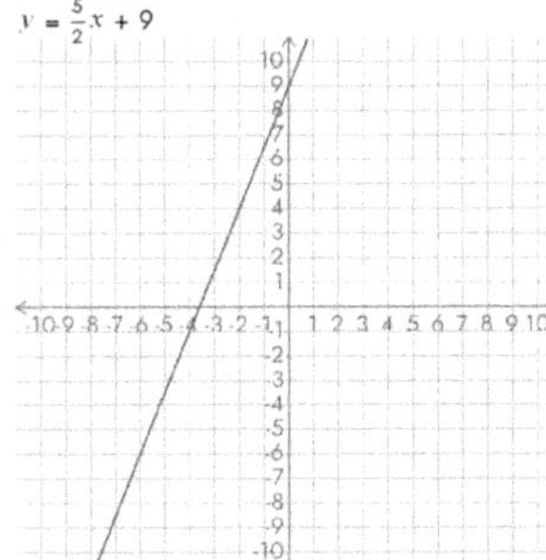